praise for *All the Dead Are Holy*

All The Dead Are Holy is, at once, a prayer, a history, and a family album. Levy unlocks secret passages into the past and unearths the artifacts of not just an extended family but whole generations of people doing their best to be who they are in a world that often wishes they were otherwise. Delivered in skillfully wrapped packages of prosody, *All the Dead Are Holy* is a wide-awake walk down memory lane in the city of what it means to be fully human.

— JodiAnn Stevenson, author of *The Procedure* and *Diving Headlong Into A Cliff Of Our Own Delusion*

This is a touching collection of reminiscences about family and ancestry that compels us to ask "Who is not my neighbor, and who remains?" This book is important because today the world is "questioning if strangers belong," and its pages provide a true, heartfelt answer. Lovely, lovely book. Truly timely in the important matters it forces one to consider.

— Adrienne (Lewis) Wright, author of *Coming Clean* and *Compared to This*

These evocative poems glow with a vitality that interweaves the personal with the collective past. They render with keen observation and fresh insight both victims and perpetrators of the Holocaust, but also portray with humor and compassion our contemporary life, where the living emerge into history.

— Skip Renker, author of *Sifting the Visible* and *Bearing the Cast*

Each of Levy's poems reads like a facet of an Ideal Cut diamond. Light glints and prisms throughout this collection, reflecting his signature wit and wisdom out into the world.

— Michael Somers, author of *Starved*

Levy's message sings a song of compassion and understanding, be they poems of navigating family relationships or poems that look unflinchingly at the history of the Holocaust, always asking us to remember, remember, remember.

— Jeff Vande Zande, author of *American Poet*

A good poem has three qualities: powerful imagery, perfect word choices, and engagement of the heart of the reader. The poems in Larry Levy's collection *All the Dead Are Holy* do just that. Evocative, engaging, and smoothly written, Mr. Levy's poems are like those wonderful rich scents in a grandmother's kitchen that you can't help but inhale as deeply as you can so you don't miss any of it.

— Philip Done, author of *32 Third Graders and One Class Bunny* and *The Ornament Box*

All the Dead Are Holy

All the Dead Are Holy

poems by **Larry Levy**

Atmosphere Press

Published by Atmosphere Press

Cover image "Milkweed" by Rob Hyner
hynerphotoart.com

Cover design by Nick Courtright
nickcourtright.com

10 9 8 7 6 5 4 3 2 1

All the Dead Are Holy
2017, Larry Levy

atmospherepress.com

Contents

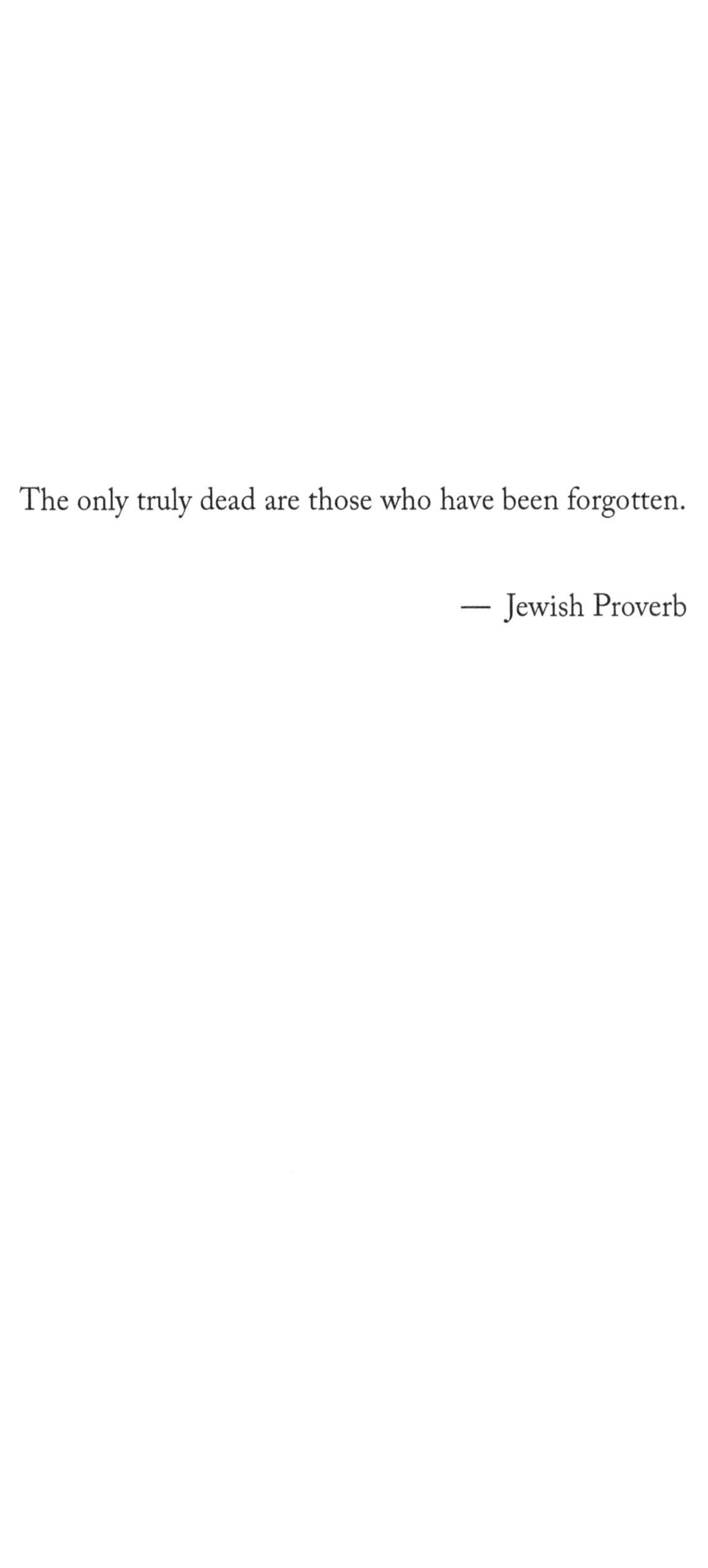

The only truly dead are those who have been forgotten.

— Jewish Proverb

I.
All the Dead Are Holy

The Best and Brightest

They may have been raised with Sundays,
filed into candle-lit pews, chanting entreaties
to the Divine, confessing transgressions,
immersing in ablutions, receiving absolutions;

and they may have been fixed for years
behind secular desks, reciting the great odes,
parsing ancient lines, having their ears
and thoughts boxed, copying codes

of citizenship, speaking only when called
upon. Such vessels, empty of mind
and soul, were poured into, filled
with what it means to be refined,

to now presume to know beyond doubt,
in the deep core, in the patriot heart,
what is best and true, having never been there
(especially if one has never been there!) —

especially if reasoning means to swear
to God knows who is fit, who is pure,
who is not my neighbor, and who remains,
and who will be herded into trains.

We Did Not Know

Savoir and *connaître* wrote historian Walter Laqueur—

on one hand there's knowing the wall is beige
the floor scuffed, the kind of knowing without wonder
without eyes welling over, that something is true

but not true like the penitent's cry for God's sake
not true like the bullet piercing the heart of a deer
in a clearing, the deer jolted awake.

That other knowing gasps at a secret made plain—
easing into a tub and the tub overflowing
or flying a kite and touching the key

or a family claiming not to know where the neighbors are—
the one-legged veteran, the toddler with doll and comb—
as they move into their now vacant home.

In the Tiergarten, 1933

Captive bears, exotic beasts,
sun on rocks, doze in moats.
Other predators storm the streets
in brown shirts and black coats,

lightning on the upper arm,
razors in the teeth and glance.
Underlings, in uniform
step, salute in a trance.

Aristocrats and sages
genuflect to broken crosses.
Jailers landscape tiger cages
with blood-red mosses,

renovating windows and doors
with imperatives for omnivores:
Exit the park! Off the bus—
with the minuscule percent of us.

Offspring of selected breeds—
wiry, well-schooled, pale—
slice weaklings from the herds,
circling until they fail.

Where is their childhood God
now, and does He weep?
Their parents stroll the promenade
at twilight, half-asleep.

Theresienstadt Kinderheim, 1944

When Ruth unpacked her stuffed cat,
the older girls called her that.
Fishka hid it in Helena's sack,
but when *Kitty* cried, she gave it back.

Helga packed her diary and rings,
the rings confiscated at the gate.
They took from us so many things
we loved, barking to cooperate.

That first night, my skin
felt sad where the ring had been,
my belly empty, the bed sagging
with straw. Someone turned, moaning,

my blanket's not soft like Auntie's goat.
I wrapped myself in Papa's winter coat.
I heard Poppinka pray, Hana beg
for home, my leg brushing a stranger's leg.

We groomed for lice, scrubbed the dirt.
Through a narrow window we saw art
in muddy fields, a faraway hill.
We sketched and sang our dreams until

Miss Friedl, Mr. Klein, most of the cast
assembled on the platform at last,
until the afternoon the train
brought the curtain down.

Last Synagogue in Warsaw

From the bus, foreign guests
shuffle in, lining the back wall.
A guide gestures toward the East,
covering her hair with a borrowed shawl.

A wartime home for pure bred
stallions, this little room
now serves graying heads,
the squinting and nearly mute.

They murmur, a kind of praying,
huddling in scarred pews,
bowing and swaying
with the long memory of Jews.

The rabbi offers Sabbath wine.
An elder kisses his tattered book,
chanting to the Divine—
his Redeemer and his Rock.

Another offers an upturned palm:
Please, help a widow with a coin.
A tourist captures her on film,
then hurries to join his line

before the *Amen*. One by one,
indistinguishable in the night,
closing valves of attention like stone,
some file to the left and some to the right.

At The Dead Sea

The sun blazed in a sky so bright
it hurt. He knelt, the water shallow.
Tried to swim, his eyes on fire.
Floated on his back, arms outspread.
There were no shells, no fish, nothing alive,
but the sea would not let him sink.

The Germans arrived, nearly naked,
their bodies generous, voices loud
with singing and holidays,
eyes hidden behind dark glasses.
Soon, their backs and bellies glowed.

Mothers, fathers, elders, children—
all slathered with healing mud, laughing.
When it dried, they looked like stone,
like clay set to be fired in a kiln
and polished like bleached bone.

A Quiet Neighbor

After the War, haggard, poor,
he petitioned to relocate
from barbed wire to fresh air.
He needed to resuscitate,

sever his memory. On his knees
he tended his garden, weeding
red potatoes, climbing peas,
his palms caked, bleeding

from blackberry thorns.
You enjoy growing a lot?
my son asked. *Where did you learn?*
Es ist ganz gut,

he smiled, *all good.*
He chopped wood,
laid brick, trimmed hedges,
renovating our neighborhood.

For all his rough edges—
sledgehammer fists, dense tongue—
he counted the Sabbath offering,
slipped shiny coins to the young,

lit candles with the suffering,
hummed hymns with the choir.
So it was no small surprise
when advocates, a survivor,

claimed he is no saint
but Kapo of Lies,
the Kommandant's banal acolyte.
Once he borrowed eggs

to bake Easter bread
for widows. Now he begs
understanding, hanging his head:
What they ordered me, I did.

Ghetto Fighters' Museum, Tel Aviv

זכור

The model of Treblinka takes up half the room,
with its toy train, archway, scale barracks,
barbed fences, smokestacks.

The soldiers in sand-colored uniforms,
blousy pants tucked into black boots,
settle their machine guns and knapsacks

on the floor, straddling the benches,
boys and girls really, their dark *sabra* eyes
checking one another's looks.

The instructor calls them to attention
in the modern secular Hebrew,
his lesson focusing on the tracks

arriving from every city and village
to this spot. *Here* he says, pointing,
their names were entered into books,

a number burned on their arms,
our brothers and sisters—
Poles, Hungarians, Greeks, Czechs—

A recruit yawns. She's heard it before.
Another checks his watch, and another
keeps looking toward the door.

The instructor notices, too,
and lowers his voice to a whisper:
You must remember. Zachor.

Home School Lessons

She greets a non-believer in the vegetable aisle
near the green tomatoes and spring greens.
She adds *God bless you*, and in single file
her daughters follow, willowy in their teens.

Their dresses brush the tops of their shoes,
covering their arms, buttoned at the neck.
They blush like rose bouquets,
remaining as silent, until asked to speak.

Each offers her name and small hand,
God blessing him, too, averting their eyes.
Mom says they stock their roadside stand
with peaches and cream corn and berries,

rising before dawn, picking all day,
keeping the books and scheduling crews.
On the Sabbath, they sing. They pray
for Israel, the conversion of the Jews.

Neighborhoods

After the War, outside the city,
homes with a den, a picture window,
arose from fields, dense and weedy.
Dad planted a poplar and a willow.

Over the garage he hung a hoop
where I practiced my winning shot.
Sundays we gathered on our stoop
as cars streamed from St. Mary's lot—

clunkers mostly, but sometimes one
would take our breath, widen our eyes,
red, convertible, a showroom shine.
We called *mine* to razzing and praise—

we second generation American kids,
Italian Catholics, Russian Jews—
but not *dagos* and never *yids*.
Sometimes we bowed in each other's pews.

Their homes smelled like onion, garlic,
and they teased me for eating pepper raw.
We ate no pork but mixed meat with milk,
following a suburban kosher law.

But downtown was asphalt, cobblestone,
tall trees cackling with mongrel birds.
My grandparents lived on Rauber Street,
a home flavored with Yiddish words,

uncles and aunts talking at once,
laughing over rich bowls of broth.
Seems like several lifetimes since
they hugged me nearly out of breath.

All Brides are Beautiful

On the back of a piece of junk mail
Cousin Freddy sketched lines—
roots, trunk, and leaves—the family tree.

There was the genius who lived in the basement,
who no one ever saw; the uncle who married
a third cousin, their children branching crooked

and bleeding; the aunt who arrived younger,
chiding her sisters for their yokel accents,
peasant myths. She was the proper Yankee,

a swinger, doing my mother's hair up
like Hollywood, like Mary Pickford;
and the playwright with a Gable mustache,

his heart seizing while trysting with a mistress.
Digging, everyone discovers a prince,
an adventurer. All the dead are holy.

Unlocked

In his dresser was a latched
cedar box. Standing on his bed
I searched it, several medals
heavy in my hand, and matched

ribbons from some life he led
in a faraway world, a war
locked within his heart, a scar
from some heroic deed,

something pure and resolute.
Downstairs, in his sleeveless tee,
he shaved while humming reveille
then drove off in his pressed suit

to a regiment of pencils and pads,
a drill of refrigerators and stoves,
the empty boxes our backyard caves
where we lay low, conducting raids

on a gang from three streets away,
scouting to commandeer their fort,
bombarding them with clods of dirt.
Once one bloodied my right eye.

At supper, when I tried to bluff,
he fixed me with his quiet face,
dressing my wound with a bag of ice.
He said nothing, but it was enough

to help me unlock my lie
for awhile, to pick at my lukewarm
meal. Tucking me in, he squeezed my arm.
I wanted to be him, a stand-up guy.

Role Model

On the shelf in the hall closet
next to his stacked fedoras
lay piles of paper, onionskin,
typewritten poems, parodies
of popular songs, the melodies
borrowed, the words a borscht
of chopped English, diced Yiddish.

When did he write these? A down time
at work? At night after we mouthy kids
were tucked in? God, we were loud!
A wonder he had a coherent thought!
A wonder he didn't have a *dreye kopf!*
Amazing I spun meaning from his puns—
The *mamaloshen* was for the grown-ups,

reserved for what we were not to hear.
But I did hear, we all heard,
and around the dinner table
we parlez vous-ed what Mel Brooks
once called *no known language*:
Lodz, Odessa, Lake Ontario,
hands, teeth, and spilled milk.

And I wonder what became
of that *megillah*, all that cleverness.
Today he'd be 100. Never smoked,
enjoyed an occasional Manhattan,
died of a stroke, quick as his wit.
I hear him laughing at his own jokes,
never at a loss for words.

His

He would want you to have these, she said,
touching his dress pants, her eyes red.
Shirts and ties lay folded on the bed,
suits in the closet smelling of Dad.

I pictured him in the cashmere coat,
Mom's *Evening in Paris* warm where
blood pulsed in her smooth throat,
a breeze ruffling her dark hair.

Take, she said, touching my arm.
Last week these were cut to his own
length and breadth, his breathing form.
But I could not even try one on.

Ideals

My mother smoked for forty years,
my father once gave in to tears,

and once I think I may have lied
dodging a consequence I feared.

My brother's marriages have died,
and years have passed without a word

from our sister, who preferred
to blame us all for what occurred

within our home. Or so she said.
Is it possible she misread,

blamed the dealer for her deal?
But how clear is any take

on all the fallibilities that make
our memories not quite ideal?

Who blew out candles on her cake,
and snuffed the recollections of

Dad's bathroom jokes, Mom's earnest love,
and picnics at the weedy lake?

Joseph Avenue

We entered Wittenberg's Deli,
Bubbie pulling a cart on wheels.
I chattered in my Yankee slang,
as she shopped the afternoon sales,

teasing in her mother tongue.
The butcher gave me a slice
of pastrami, and Mr. Kravetz
slipped me a coin, pinching my face,

calling me *little shaygetz, little prince.*
Outside, the streets were alive
with people hurrying and cars smoking,
but I held her hand and felt brave.

In her cart sat a chicken,
its face fierce and resigned,
feathers a fiery orange and red.
Now and then it complained

in a throaty twilight voice.
He won't hurt you, she said,
but in the back yard, blood
shot a foot from its missing head.

Later, we welcomed the *Shabbos*-
the warm *challah*, poppy seeds on top,
and my father's jokes, my uncle's tenor,
and her golden *luchen* soup.

Saying Grace

After the midday mourner's prayer,
we removed what we were obliged to wear,
the leather boxes and fringed shawl
that so amused my Catholic friend,
and bellied up to get our fill

of fatty soup and peppered meat,
the sharp, dark rye; the blend
of pickles, half sour, half sweet;
the wine that connoisseurs find
cloying. I sipped it warm and straight.

Will you daven with me, Cousin?
Natey asked, nodding into words
ancient and holy, his eyes closed.
I put my sandwich down, joining in,
mumbling along where memory failed.

While ten male voices filled the air,
the women in the kitchen wailed
for Grandpa gone the day before,
gone on an errand when he fell
dead before he hit the street.

Now, as through a mist,
we chanted for wine, for the dead,
the heroic Steps, the crowded port,
the café poets, Natey's eyes moist
with stories like his shirt cuffs, frayed

with use: *Ah, Odessa was the best,*
he said, *and here we are surely bereft.*
But, someone replied, *they all left*
with forged names. It's true, he sighed.
If it were so good they would have stayed.

II.
Not Even Past

Her First Day

Mom washed her oatmeal face.
Dad brushed her mop of black hair.
Her brothers ran around the kitchen
until leaving time. *Come here*

the older one said, and up the leafy street
they went, then down the slides,
singing *See, see, see playmate.*
At the bell their separate grades

beckoned. She hesitated at her door.
The older one said *Remember…behave*
and then was gone. Her teacher
said *we don't cry when we are five.*

She was shown her square on the rug.
She was taught the single file walk.
She put on her listening ears for story time
and waited to be called on to speak.

At the Mall

Electric, this child
spins past my bench.

A vein of gold,
nimble as a finch.

Her black shoes clap
on the turquoise tile.

A Cinderella slip-
sliding at the Ball.

Gum-soled walkers,
arms like metronomes,

count laps, lock lockers,
ears to their phones.

But she riffs in the key
of Augmented Me.

Her ensemble ablaze—
the full spectrum's rays.

Today she dressed
herself to step out—

Queen of the Fest.
Let other kids pout,

yanking grown-up arms
out of their sockets,

groveling like worms
for pennies in pockets.

In her diamond crown,
ribbons, spit curls,

ankle bells, gauzy gown—
she sings, she twirls.

Friday, Walking Home

She found a pine sprig, a cone,
and one dandelion ablaze, alone

under the gooseberry, a prickly spot.
And lying dead in violets, what

may have been a mouse or mole,
paw prints near, nearby its hole.

She thought on all of this awhile—
do blossoms and berries have a soul

as she'd heard about all living creatures?
Was the world God's or was it Nature's?

She plopped pebbles in a shallow pool,
wondering if the world was kind or cruel.

Or maybe things happened just because.
Maybe without reasons it just was.

She cradled a blue and broken shell
to discuss on Monday during show-and-tell.

Sidekick

I.

I galloped around the house, holster
and pistol at my side, boots clicking
the pavement. My brother
lurched from the bushes, sticking
me with his plastic sword, and down
I went, Pancho hat flying, bone
on stone, wailing. *Go on,*
you baby. Go on home,
he hollered at my limping form
disappearing into the house.
Minutes later I returned, ice
on my elbow, band-aid on my
nose. He stared full in my face.
Nice try, he said. *Nice try.*

II.

He threw the hardball high as the roof.
I circled below on wobbly feet,
holding up my boondoggle mitt.
Catch it, he said, trying not to laugh.
The ball seemed to hang by a thread,
small and glowing like an early star,
growing larger and more clear
as it descended toward my head,
glancing off the feeble web,

conking me a good one near my eye,
raising a yelp, a purplish knob.
But I would not cry.
I would not run away.
Nice try, he said. *Nice try.*

Champions

While parents bundle in folding chairs, boys
warm their cleats, first right then left,
their bodies all rubber bands, their feet deft

with the ball. They are good at making noise,
high-pitched fox yips in the morning air.
Now they move into sunlight, legs bare

from the hem to the knees.
They are all in black and feel mean,
scooting along the pitch from line to line

without stumbling, without slipping on the freeze
that settled overnight on the grass and stands
where moms clutch mugs in both hands

exhaling clouds of pleasure, of praise,
while dads bark *get your head in the game.*
Then the smallest, leaping, boots one home,

and the referee whistles autumn days
to a close. The boys laugh at every bruise
believing they will never lose.

Poetry Lesson

Becky slouches at her desk,
one of a cluster of four.
Across from her is Cameron,
hair moussed into a Mohawk,
body taut as a bowstring.

To her left, Alexander,
ripe with milk fat;
to her right, a girl years
from changes that will play
havoc on her body and mind.

But Becky has already begun
the first leg of that round trip,
is packing light so far
but may have to pay extra
for the luggage.

Now she stares a thousand miles
at the wall, ceiling, window
or in a mirror, the album
of her mind, where the camera
scrolls shots of her dog, who

she rolled a ball, fed, buried;
or of her brother, pulling her hair,
crawling into her stuff, pushing
her cell phone's buttons, arriving
like these pictures, without permission.

Jump in the Line

He has not selected marble from the quarry
to carve away what is not Moses. He has not
gazed into blinding sunflowers, the twilight

despair of crows, nor rowed the one-way ferry
across the dark river. He is not guided
by Virgil, nor has he abandoned all hope.

Every Monday, a few minutes after our teacher
hits play on her boom box, and the regulars begin
the warm up of heads, shoulders, knees, and toes,

he enters, squinting toward the light,
hand on his guide's shoulder, whooping
the high notes with Belafonte, with Shakira.

He cannot see the old women smiling
or the younger ones raising eyebrows.
No matter the song's volume, he is louder.

He greets, apologizing for being late.
He cha-chas, excusing himself, to his favorite spot.
He does not stop talking. Or laughing.

He is not Pavarotti, climbing the scale.
He is not Baryshnikov, leaping to the rafters.
He was never a small boy in the islands.

He does not samba on a Brazilian beach,
a bronze body amidst nearly naked women.
Rather, he jumps in the line, rocks his body in time,

shorts slipping below his plump belly and cheeks.
He saves his last, best dance for the ladies.
OK, they believe him.

Goddess in 7th Grade

Kids exploded from the bus.
You stood out in the stampede,
electric with your raucous
teeth, 'fro a thunderhead,

one sock green, the other red,
laces loose on high-top sneaks,
swearing a rival was dead,
terrorizing whites, blacks,

and anyone in between—a first
shove on the stairs, a vow
to beat a butt at lunch, a fist
in Jackie's chest, a lower blow

to Andre—no one was safe
from you back then—loud
child, angry as a knife,
and I must have been mad

thinking I could be a friend—
I, your teacher, facing your tongue
every day, wishing your mood
brighter, and so often wrong.

But somehow we got along,
despite your detentions and bulging file.
You spoke in upper case slang,
flashing me one eye, a fiery will:

You know you love me, Mister Man.
You know I'm Best Kid in your class.
Goddess, somehow I was your fan,
a witness to your large and losing cause.

My Catholic Girl

He wanted to pin a rose on the strap
of her gown, but his hands
hovered like wrens afraid to light.
She smiled *Let me help,*
showing him how to do it right.

They were juniors, their first prom.
He wanted her to think him clever.
He wanted to exhale and be calm
but staggered, unsteady as a sailor
new to the sea's swell and storm.

He prayed she would draw him closer.
Then she took him to Midnight Mass.
During Communion, when he tried to feel
for her hand, she made the Sign of the Cross.
She taught him when to kneel,

swallow the wafer, sip the wine.
She whispered *Just do what I do.*
And that night, he followed her lead,
sharing something powerful and new—
surely the body and blood Divine.

Saints and Virgins

According to the guidebook, Iglesia de Santo Domingo
Is *the finest example of colonial architecture in Oaxaca.*
To escape the purgatory of midday heat,
the noon sun as bright as revelation, we step quietly inside,
enveloped in the cool dark of the sanctuary.

Neither of us Catholic, we neither bow
nor dip our fingers in the water nor genuflect,
but sit in the nearest and most vacant pew.
Slowly our eyes widen. The entire church is vacant
save for a few women, also alone in their pews,

perhaps with their supplications and gratitude,
and everyone is silent. The silence is as profound
as prayer. I can almost hear the words rising
to the dome, to its millions of intricate designs,
and to the golden likenesses of the virgins and saints.

Perhaps the statue of Domingo hears the hearts
of the old women kneeling. Perhaps Guadalupe,
her delicate head tilted slightly, is listening.
I cannot say for sure. I grew up across the street
from St. Margaret Mary Church. Neighborhood

kids attended their school but still swiped candy
from the corner store, still muttered *Jesus Christ*
when offended or surprised. Once my friend's mother,
overhearing, scolded *Andrew, don't take the Name
Of the Lord in vain!* I had no idea what she meant

and never set foot inside the church or spoke to the nuns.
Now we take a few pictures with our iPad, flashless
in order not to offend anyone, least of all Jesus,
Domingo or Guadalupe. Leaving, we notice
kids in the plaza, each wearing the stunning red or blue

or immaculate black or white uniforms of their collegio.
Around the fountain, boys laugh loudly. Under tall trees,
girls smile with perfect teeth, whispering and glancing.
On a bench, in the shadow of a laurel, a couple kiss,
unaware of anything but each other's warm face.

A Guy I Knew Once

He wasted little time in bed
or minding any teacher's rule.
Awake at witching hours instead
he skulked behind the school.

Some things he never said,
belly to belly, the intercourse rock,
cruising the shore, the submarine races,
guffawing in classmates' faces.

Better to sneer, to mock,
better to howl than swallow crow.
Laying rubber around the block,
pushing until it came to shove.

Many things he never said.
He knew nobody lived above
hammering his heart and head.
Suspecting someone dwelled below,

he wasted little time on love,
knowing he was in the know.

In The Neighborhood

Walter Scott, in pressed shirts, striped ties,
wrote his name at the top of each page,
the vowels round and the *W* large,
a single stroke through the double tees.

He walked with a hitch, like all his boys,
wore a poofy 'fro where he stored his pick.
That's how it was in that school in those days
where many were sent home or called in sick

or walked the hall with smoldering faces,
belts unbuckled, cruising for a fight.
But Walter shined his shoes and tied his laces,
and in his essays spelled words right.

He packed a copy of *Ivanhoe*,
saw his gallant self in the Black Knight.
His neighbors, not Saxon nor Norman quite,
quarreled often, laid each other low.

But Walter was OK with Bloods or Crips.
He said every neighborhood was his home.
He showed it in class when he crossed the room
with his wise guy smile, his sidelong quips.

Once another teacher wrote him up.
He missed his bus, needed a lift,
directed me across town, right, then left,
then for some reason told me *stop*

in a voice I could hardly hear.
He said, *Hey, thanks for the ride,*
entering an alley with no house near,
toward the Projects where so many died.

My Teacher

Ancient, short, plump,
Guadalcanal vet. *Deaf as a stone*
he shrugged, tapping his hearing aid,
cupping his better ear like a telephone
whose wires were badly frayed.

He squinted over the podium
toward me, the mumbling back row boy,
or noted a lump of a girl, transparent
by the window, seeking a way
to draw each of us out

of our adolescent agony
and into the realm of Faulkner's Gavin
facing his neighbors' raised voices
with the kind of response—calm reason—
that he championed. *You have choices*

Mr. Levy, he said, reminding me
that Hamlet's time, however out of joint,
was the only time he had.
He was always asking, *Who has a point?*
But whatever I thought I rarely said,

slumping in my seat instead,
working hard to be cool, as if in a trance.
You can sleep or you can take a stand,
he coaxed. *Come on. Take a chance.*
Lacking conviction, I raised my hand.

Volunteer

That sixteenth summer, on a dare
he swam across the river where
it flowed northward to the lake—
the lake that sometimes made him sick
with rashes red as poison oak.
Still, he dove into the slick,

shouting to friends *Geronimo*,
and immediately felt an undertow
dragging him down, his breath
quickening as he sliced the waves,
inhaling water in his nose and mouth—
it was what he knew of being brave,

sprinting headlong without a trace
of fear, feeling full of grace.
At the far pier, he clambered up
panting, bursting into a laugh,
waving, boasting like a champ.
Oh, he was blushing with life.

On a dare, he learned to iron
his creases, hunt alone
in a fog, disappear in a swamp.
In desert drab, his schoolboy face
smudged, he ignored sleep,
stalking strangers in a dark place.

And when he died a few years
later, drowning in blood and tears,
teachers recalled his ready smile.
His pastor praised his righteous pride.
Coach knew he'd gone the extra mile
to win the colors for our side.

Guide to Belfast

After the truce, murals of the war
greet tourists driving everywhere.

Not long before, Falls Road
determined if wine was wine or blood.

Those whose colors ran orange or green
despised or sang *God Save Our Queen.*

Is it over, the fusillade? Is it even past—
mothers pushing infant carriages at last;

churchgoers invoking the Jesus they adore
without Semtex exploding through the door;

university students reading Heaney, Muldoon;
lovers strolling cemeteries in late afternoon?

With maps, they come from many lands
to weep where they lay Bobby Sands.

They hit pubs with fiddlers, tip a pint,
sing off-key verses to their Saint.

I drive the bus, sometimes want to shout
For Christ's sweet sake, what was it about?

In the Marketplace

Morning, evening, he appears
bearing woven souvenirs,

wooing with a wicker dog,
iguana, elephant, or frog.

He urges us to oink or touch.
I do not need the pig that much.

A viejo offers birdseed cake.
His mom, a many-jointed snake.

A revolucionario
can't comprehend, but won't take no.

I am unsure how else to say
No me gusta Fidel o Che.

No more Kahlo reproductions.
No more Zocalo seductions.

Kid after kid with nuts and gum
insistent that I purchase some.

This isn't what I came here for.
Please, nada más. Please, por favor.

Survival Training

This morning while filling my cart with bottles of wine,
apples, a jar of honey, and whatever else was on the list,
a man I had not seen in years called my name,
your old soccer coach, and asked about you.

He said his daughter had been home over Christmas
and recalled being in a musical with you one summer
now more than twenty years ago, when you sat
surrounded by teenage girls

in her backyard in the cool evenings after rehearsals,
charming them all with your smile, curly hair,
tall, lean frame, and your stories of survival training,
including eating worms and crickets,

and how you winked at the girls' squeals of dismay
and delight and, lifting a rock, uncovered a beetle,
black and hard-shelled, skittering with its wicked legs,
and popped it in your mouth.

The coach recalling this was smiling, and I smiled back,
even when I told him we had not heard from you in years,
that you had cut us all off, family and old friends alike.
I said all this while smiling

though I confessed it was especially hard on your mother
who blames herself, and how I, too, every day
think of you, of what I might have done differently.
The coach put his hand on my shoulder

said he was sorry to hear this, that such behavior
sounded the opposite of how he remembered you,
a boy filled with sweetness. So this is the face I choose
to present to the world, smiling,

as if my life is filled with sweetness, too,
as if it is all honey and apples and wine,
more than a little wine in the evenings now,
to ease the black shell around my heart.

Making the Team

The list taped to the gym door,
his name missing, hurt like a knife.
If not basketball, what was he for?
What was to come of his 10th grade life?

Twelve uniforms. He was number thirteen,
perched in the stands in dungarees,
rooting for blue and gold, his sign
celebrating the names of other guys,

friends with muscle, agility, height.
He had a left hand, long-range pop,
obvious heart, but too much weight
to fool anyone with his start and stop.

After moping for days, on a whim
he wandered into the high school pool,
discovering the distance swim
suited a point guard built like a seal.

But not right away. That first week,
thrashing the repeats, lungs burning,
he thought he'd drown or die on the deck.
Then his times dropped. He was learning

silence, patience, mile after mile,
rhythm itself becoming his goal.
Breathe, reach, rotate, exhale—
sustenance for his soul.

Winning Season, 1964

Though under six feet tall,
he jumped center for our team,
rising impossibly for a loose ball.
Teachers and students knew his name—

it hung in rafters for every game.
They chanted it the morning after,
woofing, rapping in clever rhyme
over the school PA, to much laughter

and hand jiving—he had it all,
our champion, our soul mate,
the only black kid in the school,
everyone's brother, no girl's date.

First Date at the L & K

She sits across from him in the booth
taking small bites of a cinnamon bun
steaming between them.

She sips her milk while he reads
his poem about Michael Fury,
the Irish boy who died for love.

Well, this one's different, she thinks.
He isn't trying to get me drunk
and so far his green eyes look into mine

as if he believes I understand Joyce.
It's almost 11:00 PM, and they're starting
to put the empty chairs on top of the tables,

and the waiter is mopping the floor
back by the telephone and rest rooms.
A few cars drive slowly by in the dark,

but her mind is racing
with something substantial here,
something transparent.

Who is he really, this boy
whose hamburger is getting cold
while he reads? Maybe she'll marry him.

She already asks him with her eyes
to be for her what she thinks he is,
one who will talk with her in the dark.

Maybe they'll be married for decades.
Does she have any idea what she silently
offers him? *Yes*, she thinks. *I will. Yes.*

III.
Now We Are Here

Evening Stroll

Do sidewalk beggars make any money?
Does anybody give a centavo to this woman,
her face like sun-beaten leather,
hand like a chicken's claw?

This family, too, tonight, a young mother,
baby in her lap, boy holding a plastic cup
to passers-by in the Alcala, father playing
the same accordion tune over and over—

and the cup empty. How are they here?
How do we pass by and not see? Or do see,
waving a clean, empty palm, perfunctory
no, gracias, continuing our conversation

on the way to Las Danzantes for postre.
Don't do it, we are advised. They are actors—
stooped posture, hangdog head,
high and hungry pitch. *Si, sí*, we reply.

But we have worked with actors, have
also acted on stage, and if these viejos,
these *little duffers*, as Cheryl calls them,
are acting, we willingly suspend disbelief,

a peso offering a momentary stay
against guilt, if not confusion.
Moments later, we spoon flan de la noche,
a guitarist singing of *alma y corazón*.

Twilight Run

Phlox lines the river trail—
white, purple, and in-between.
Between the stream and springy soil—
green and darker green.

Between the shadows and aging sun—
a turtle sleeping on a stone,
a silver flash of silver fin,
a small rain.

In my feet an ancient hurt
betrays a fire in the heart.
A hawk blazes above the trees
with burning eyes.

Birches glow in a dense field—
foxglove, thistle, burr and dock.
Between the gray and cloudy cold—
dark and more dark.

My Sixties

If you remember, you weren't there,
the saying goes, but I was there,
drug-free except for testosterone
and polite except for scruffy hair.
Just a kid, renting to own.

Talkin' 'bout my generation,
the song went, but they weren't me.
My roomie honored the First of May,
hummed *The Internationale* off-key
and was ready to die.

Another wanted to bomb Hanoi
or waste Fonda. Afternoons over beer
his lectures began *Now, in the Nam…*
Oh he was ready to go to war
or warm the room.

I couldn't go to Stockholm,
march in a line, or paint my face.
You belong to a Gang of One,
a buddy argued, because
everybody had to align.

But at commencement I was alone.
I remember salvos
left and right of the speaker's views.
I remember how they fogged the air.
And soon after, I paid dues,

ready or not, assigning my name
to obligations, complicated and unclear.
I was a wanderer—who knew where? —
spending on lay-away, buying time.
Now in my sixties, the decades blur.

One friend dozes in a shuffleboard home.
Another walks midnight halls in fear.
One spends afternoons at the bar,
and one's a bottle brimming with blame.
Once we were there, and now we are here.

Unsafe At Any Speed

We sat in my mother's '64 Corvair, motor idling in neutral,
parked in front of Paul's clapboard cottage in White City,
so called because the neighborhood once was nothing

but canvas tents on the bluff overlooking Ontario,
on the eastern side of the mouth of the Genesee,
flowing north, lifeline of the Iroquois and the city of Rochester.

It was past midnight, but under the full summer moon
the lake shone, the long pier stretching into the darkness.
We turned the radio down,

songs about loving the one you're with,
so Paul, who had neither car nor license
nor much of a singing voice, and was sitting there

filling the passenger seat to overflowing,
could warm to a story, rev his engine, blow out the carbon,
and Mitchell sat in the back, full of throaty commentary,

and Oh My Gods, chumming the water,
casting Paul starter possibilities to see what lunker
might rise from the depths, might take the hook.

Mitchell said, "If I told you that a year to the day
after I died you were to come to the end of that pier
at midnight, and I'd be there, what would you do?"

"OK," Paul began, "I'd put on my best suit,
the one I got for my uncle's funeral, my black tie
with silver paisley, my Italian shoes, well-shined,

and I'd get a bowler hat, wear it at an angle,
very British, and a silver-tipped cane,
and I'd stroll the half mile of the pier to the very end,

and there I'd light my pipe, you know, enjoy a bowl."
"You wouldn't be scared?" Mitchell asked.
"Not a bit," Paul said, "I'd be curious. Why not?"

"And if you heard something wash up to the pier
and start to rise out of the waves?"
"Well, then, I suppose I'd get the hell out of there

as fast as my ass would carry me."
We laughed so hard the car shook.
"Well," Mitchell said, "I don't expect to die for awhile."

And Paul said, "If you keep driving with Levy
in this Corvair, you never know. Hell, I'm taking my life
in my hands just riding in the death seat here."

After high school we sometimes fishtailed,
sometimes caught dry pavement.
Mitchell died young and alone

in an unheated hut somewhere in Wales.
Paul never wrote the play we thought he had in him.
A few years ago, while checking out at a grocery,

he nearly checked out for good.
I learned this when, after years of silence,
he wrote me handwritten advice—

he never typed, phoned, or used a computer—
to travel safely, listen to the music,
and love the one you're with.

Cold Fall Morning

Even with the field so blanketed with hoar frost
I couldn't see the far end line or penalty box,
the game went on, to the delight of the Skywalkers,
their blue tees and socks stark against the white-on-white
grass, trees, and sky. Even so, they all wore shorts—

Toe, Flash, Hulk, Leadfoot, Little Vince,
and Big Vince, too, my right hand, who seemed immune
to November's dawn gales, and set the example
for all except Jared, whose sweats were already soaked
and dragging about his ankles.

In the fog, I penciled a lineup with a numb hand.
Younger sisters jumped in circles, chanting *Fire up!*
while the rest of the families breathed little clouds
of talk, huddling, wrapped in blankets.
I clapped along to keep the blood moving.

Our opponents, swaddled in mittens and leggings,
waddled Gumby-like in irregular lines,
stiff, stumbling, tripping, as if awoken
in the dark suddenly older and afflicted
with snow blindness or frostbite.

Big Vince loped from sideline to sideline,
coaxing one boy to use his left, another the instep.
He warmed up our keeper with shots
to all corners of the net. He patted many backs.
Throughout the game he paced, cheeks glowing.

Some thirty years later, it suddenly seems
the boys patrol their own sidelines in other towns
around the Midwest. Vince stops by occasionally,
whispers *hermano*, takes my right arm
to steady himself from the cold he cannot kick.

The Veteran

He limps, even with a cane,
his younger wife on his other arm,
and wears long pants, a jacket,
even though it's plenty warm,

and the talk flutters around him,
the laughter, a line of song.
We hum, recalling the rhyme,
but he does not sing along.

We prompt him a bit,
posing a question here,
changing the subject there,
his wife smoothing his thin hair.

Suddenly he mentions the War,
the crashing near Suribachi with
his crew, and the shelling's
thunder, screams, the death

everywhere that day decades
ago, as if even in this Florida café
it is still clear, still happening,
though his eyes seem far away.

And I imagine him a teen still,
shouting orders, eyes wide,
his body taut and trained,
and everyone terrified

but alive. He recalls
his long career, his first wife.
We exchange smiles,
a small laugh.

He is sorry we have to go.
He is sorry about his faint voice.
He stumbles a step
after our embrace.

Estate Sale

Thistles and dock and shoots of red bud
poke through the white stone mulch,
elbowing her daisies and gentian,

while we haul the last bubble-wrapped
treasures labeled in sturdy boxes:
the rainbow artistry of children,

the photos of fair weather voyages,
infant curls and news clippings curled
like punch lines with frequent re-telling,

and the Easter bulletins, the Grand Openings,
the sipped sharp bourbon, sweet vermouth,
and the unopened gifts of Spanish port.

Because she walked with purpose,
humming soprano with her radio hymns,
and ate spring greens and red plums,

we supposed she would outlive us all.
Months later, we continue to sift
her middens like an archeological dig.

Finally the rooms, smelling of floral
cleansers, open vast and silent
for the next tenant's dreams and sorrows.

Before closing the last door,
we cull a rake, a plate, heirloom
primroses, trillium, blue bells

and take bets on what will disappear
first from the things piled curbside.
Next morning we see we guessed wrong.

On Her Terms

When the nuggets lay uneaten
in the dish in the kitchen corner,
and she could no longer
limp up the back stairs,
we decided to lay her burden down.

She lay in my lap on the drive to the vet.
No caterwauling or climbing the upholstery.
She slumped asleep on the shiny table
as Dr. White applied the necessary dose,
the assistant weeping. She knew her

before she was weaned and through
spaying and annual weigh-ins. We buried
her in the hosta garden where
on the warmest days she often sought
refuge from the hunt. Odd, old thing,

now gone to cool dust and worms.
In her prime, she shadowed me around
the yard, her surrogate parent, singing to me
while I murmured from my childhood
half-remembered Hebrew melodies,

Peace be with you, peace be with you.
Now I recited the equally distant
prayer over the dead, *Yisgadol,*
Vi-yiskadosh…intended for humans,
and probably sacrilegious to recite

over a lowly black house cat. But, I reasoned
on faith: she was—who knows?—maybe
one of God's elect, a champion
of joy and play. Well, *where be
your jibes now?* I wondered the next day,

when two wingless young men arrived,
black bearded and robed, angels intent
on returning me to the *tefillin*, to chant
prayers of gratitude for Holy Creation.
Mourning in my own way, I begged out.

Elegy for Chooch

A slight bleed on the brain
said the nurse, but really none
is slight. Your right arm gone.
Gone your omelette puns,

your sunny side. The yolk's
on us, my brother-in-disguise.
One of your script's outtakes,
your Creator cracking wise.

How many summer days
with bat, mitt, ball,
the neighborhood guys?
The banter was all.

Now under a summer sky
chirp one hundred birds,
but when will you and I
play catch with words?

Pictures

Before I was born, my mother
glued snapshots in her scrapbook,
the four cornered narrative of a life,
all black and white, which I would look

at often. There was a bearded man
with eyes fierce and sincere,
and his large family, solemn and dark.
As a kid, I wondered who they were.

The *whole mishpucha* Mom called them.
They wore stiff collars, vests, tallises.
Great-grandma, her sisters—hens
plump-bosomed in long dresses,

their hair swept up in buns—posed
without smiles, looking strong
and solid. Their new world
spoke a cackling tongue

they never mastered, but there
they were anyway, sharing honey cake,
glasses of tea, points-of-view: meals
served with many courses of talk.

And there were their children,
adorned like little Russians,
standing between legs, riding
on shoulders, pulling someone's

hair. Then they are grown, now
smiling in one another's arms, joking
on blankets at Charlotte Beach,
picnicking in tennis whites, smoking

like 30's movie stars, all-Americans.
And finally I am there, a little prince
eating a tomato, wearing a holster,
a bulldog in my Mickey Mantle stance.

And there are my brother and sister,
their heads a cloud of healthy curls.
They are blowing out candles, bowling
at parties of chubby boys and girls.

How many are withered now, almost gone—
cold stones on their stones! When home,
haunted by pictures, I, too, place a stone
and rhyme to keep them warm.

Dia de los Muertos

Today marigolds sing to God.
Let me call them *flores de muerte*
ascending the altar of Soledad
for our family's suerte.

Let me put away workaday hurt,
prepare tamales and dress in white.
I will fold my legs under a wool skirt,
reminiscing all night

of cousins gone, the life of our Saint,
of children far away and grown.
Their souls approach. Let me anoint
their stones, for I am not alone.

A Local Habitation and a Name

When we moved into this old house
our acre was a tangle of grape vines,
creeping Charlie, shoots off old maples.
We began clearing it, spending many a day
filling dumpsters the city hauled away.

The three previous owners did the same,
neighbors said. They also chopped in earnest
before putting down the sharp tools
in favor of afternoons in lawn chairs
and long yarns over beers.

We thought we could do better,
but after decades our flower beds
lack definition. No theme steadies
them down. Here tulips, there violets,
and everywhere forget-me-nots—

all God's creations. But the eye wanders
like a hummingbird sipping sweetness
on the wing and moving quickly on.
This spring we will again bend low
deciding what to keep, what must go.

Census

Scrolling down tight lines of script,
I imagine a native recording a name,
country of origin, original tongue,

questioning if the strangers belong.
And I wonder if he slipped
in an obligatory slur of blame

about Romanians, eight to a room,
Poles with mismatched consonants,
Russians, clearing their throats,

dismissing the yokel in three coats,
whose family read the handwriting
on Old World walls: *Parasites!*

And maybe he noted birth dates
of the green-eyed kids in scruffy clothes,
yearning to riff the razzmatazz,

to jitterbug in the hall to ragtime jazz,
the hall reeking of garlic and onion.
And my mother, just a baby then,

one of the beautiful babies of 1910,
and Dad, in knickers, a Buster Brown,
studying Talmud and five card Monty.

Over the years they taught me plenty,
how to loop my Yankee name on a line,
how to breast my cards, to double down.

Someday someone might come upon
a page with my name, and discover
husband, parent, teacher, citizen, lover.

Siri Spell Checks My Poem

That word is not in my dictionary.
          Got a modifier more vivid than *very*?

Your quatrain rhymes lines two and four—
          Really? Who uses rhyme anymore?

Capitalize the first word in a sentence.
          Is your theme *guilt*? Consider *repentance*.

This cliché is for the birds.
          Are you seriously using indented words?

Why the italics? Why boldface?
          Think you're cummings, mr. lower case?

Shouldn't Cummings be capitalized?
          Perhaps everything should be revised.

This stanza may be unnecessary.
          That word is not in my dictionary.

Poets who explain have a circle in Hell.
          The way to heaven? Show, don't tell.

Quit nudging me to think or feel.
          Are you trusting details to reveal?

Are you rewarding your reader with surprise?
          This choice—do you think it wise?

Do adult readers want melodrama?
Would it kill you to use a comma?

Your whole approach is reactionary.
That word is not in my dictionary.

High School Reunion

So now we refrain from alcohol,
preferring lemonade over ice.
It's twelve steps to the banquet hall,
castanets clicking in our knees.

Once we downed three dogs at a clip,
a dozen donuts, sweet and warm.
Now, nibbling carrots and yogurt dip,
you punctuate a joke, squeezing my arm.

You recall the time I fed the pot,
your straight besting my two pair.
And how we drove the dawn streets,
windows down, wind ruffling our hair,

exaggerating that Saturday date,
rocking off-key with a radio tune.
The adult world? It could wait.
We clocked out. It was June,

the cloudless sky, the broad lake
—acres of alewife, untreated dung.
The first fifty yards were the hardest hike.
But weren't we immortal or at least young?

Now talk's less inflated, less light.
We embrace in a way we never did then,
linger over names into the night
recalling those sleeping under the dust—

the dreamer, so innocent and just;
the athlete whose sprinting took the race;
the wit, improvising the teacher's script.
I close my eyes, hearing each voice.

How many years, how many miles!
A beauty I chased now offers a kiss,
her wrinkled hand. My old friend smiles—
Cheer up, Buddy. Enjoy this.

Acknowledgements

Several of these poems appeared, sometimes in slightly different form, in the following publications:

Third Wednesday: Goddess in 7th Grade, In the Neighborhood, Home School Lessons, Ideals, Volunteer, The Quiet Neighbor, On Her Terms, A Local Habitation and a Name, Census, Evening Stroll

Postcard Poems: Dia de los Muertos

The South Carolina Review: My Catholic Girl

Meow: On Her Terms

Tenemos: Twilight Run

Many thanks to Nick Courtright for his patient and astute reading of this manuscript.

To Cheryl, wise, clever, more precious than rubies. Mi amor, mi corazón.

About the Author

Larry Levy's poems have appeared in *The Virginia Quarterly Review*, *Wyoming Review*, *Poet and Critic* (Iowa*)*, *Poet Lore* (Washington DC), *The Driftwood Review*, *Third Wednesday*, *South Carolina Review, Controlled Burn*, and other little and online magazines.

An earlier book *I Would Stay Forever If I Could and New Poems* is in a second expanded printing from Mayapple Press. He has also published *Three Things That Have Nothing to Do With Teaching,* a collection of reflective logs.

Retired from teaching at every level from pre-school to graduate school, Larry and his wife Cheryl live in Midland, Michigan where they direct plays and conduct workshops on acting and writing for the Midland Center for the Arts.

www.ingramcontent.com/pod-product-compliance
Ingram Content Group UK Ltd.
Pitfield, Milton Keynes, MK11 3LW, UK
UKHW042013190726
13854UKWH00005B/2273